Grab a Big Bag

by Olivia Perez
illustrated by Jennifer Anderson

Practice Decodable 7

McGraw Hill Education

Bothell, WA • Chicago, IL • Columbus, OH • New York, NY

MHEonline.com

Send all inquiries to:
McGraw-Hill Education
8787 Orion Place
Columbus, OH 43240

ISBN: 978-0-02-145040-4
MHID: 0-02-145040-4

Printed in China.

7 8 9 10 11 DSS 27 26 25 24 23

A girl had a bag.

Did it rip?

It did.

The girl got a big bag.

Did it rip?

It did.

The girl got a big, big bag.

It did not rip!